I Survived and So Can You!

Surviving The Spirit of Abortion, Rejection and Suicide

By

Wayne A. Smith, Sr.

ISBN 979-8-89504-536-7

This book is designed to provide accurate and authoritative information regarding the subject matter covered. This information is given with the understanding that neither the author nor LEEDS PRESS CORP is engaged in rendering legal or professional advice. The opinions expressed by the author are not necessarily those of LEEDS PRESS CORP

I Saw the Light, and then came His Voice....

The story of surviving 3 suicidal attempts.

Table of Contents

Forward

In "I Survived and So Can You: Surviving the Spirit of Abortion, Rejection, and Suicide," Bishop Wayne A. Smith invites readers on a profound and deeply personal exploration of the human experience. With raw honesty and unwavering courage, Bishop Smith shares his story of grappling with the shadows of despair and emerging on the other side with renewed purpose and faith. Through the pages of this book, readers will find solace in the author's vulnerability, strength in his resilience, and hope in his message of redemption.

As you delve into these pages, be prepared to confront the complexities of life's deepest wounds and discover the transformative power of healing and forgiveness. Bishop Smith's words serve as a guiding light for those navigating their own paths of struggle, offering a roadmap to resilience and a testament to the enduring strength of the human spirit. "I Survived and So Can You" is more than a book—it is a lifeline, a source of inspiration, and a testament to the unyielding power of hope. Embrace these pages and embark on a journey of survival, healing, and triumph.

Carlton Facey, BSc, M.Div, D.Div, D.Min.
Psychotherapist CCP- CC -DPP
Presiding Prelate International Council of Bishops &
Pastor

Tributes to the Author

"Your dedication to your craft shines brightly with each word you pen, illuminating the path to your literary dreams. Your perseverance in the face of challenges inspires me, showing the world the depth of your passion and determination. As you embark on this journey of writing your book, know that I stand beside you, cheering you on every step of the way. Your creativity knows no bounds, and I have no doubt that your book will touch the hearts and minds of readers, leaving a lasting impact for years to come."

"Embrace the joy of creation, my love, knowing that your words have the power to spark imagination, evoke emotions, and ignite change to everyone who may read them. Trust in your unique voice and vision, for it is a beacon of authenticity in a world hungry for genuine storytelling. Remember, even on the toughest days, that your talent is a gift meant to be shared with the world. With unwavering faith in your abilities and the support of those who cherish you, there is nothing you cannot achieve. Keep writing, keep dreaming, and know that I am here, believing in you every step of the way."
Your wife,
Paula Davis-Smith

The story of my father is probably one of the best stories I know. A key source of inspiration when I need it and I never get tired of hearing it. "No weapons formed against me shall prosper." This story is a true testament to that statement. People wonder why the anointing and the shine shows on my father like it does, but nobody would think the story was how it was. Just like a diamond that has to be torched and molded by the fire, God did that here; and as the story continues to be written, this book is a testament to withstanding that fire and coming out shining.

My Son- Wayne A Smith Jr

I just wanted to start off by saying how proud I am of my father. My dad has been through so much and he has taught me that no matter what, I should never give up and to always have faith. My father's journey hasn't been the easiest, but he always trusted God to pull him through. No matter what, I know my father will believe in me and I'm glad he's getting the opportunity to share his story with others.

My Daughter- Abigail Alexandria Smith

To my dear brother who I also have the privilege of calling my Bishop, Words cannot fully express the depth of gratitude and love I feel for you, my brother and guiding light in faith. You have not only been a source of strength and support in my life, but also, a beacon of hope and inspiration to all who are fortunate enough to know you. As my brother growing up, you were my leader and protecter through all the challenges we faced coming from humble beginnings. We didn't have much, but we always had each other, which was more than enough. I am so happy to see how far we have made it in life, and how it makes our mother's heart smile. I am forever grateful for the bond we share as siblings. As my Bishop, you have been a true shepherd of the flock, leading with grace, humility, and a deep commitment to serving others. I will never forget the first time I sat in your congregation and listened to you preach. It was life changing, and in that moment, I knew for sure the life I wanted to live, yet I spent many years after that running until there was nowhere else to run.

Your words of wisdom, your comforting prayers, and your acts of compassion have touched the hearts of countless individuals including myself, guiding us on a spiritual journey and helping us to find solace in times of need. Your dedication to God's work, your unwavering faith, and your tireless efforts to spread the Gospel is a testament to the extraordinary leader you are. You embody the very essence of what it means to be a servant of the Lord, and your ministry has brought light and healing to so many souls in need. I am blessed beyond measure to have you as my brother and bishop, and I am grateful to God for the gift of your presence in my life. May God continue to bless you abundantly as you continue to walk in His light and spread the Gospel. You are a true blessing and a testament to what God can do. I am honored to call you my brother and my Bishop.

With all my love and admiration,

Your African Princess

Sister- Kennie-Ann Wilson

Wayne, I'm incredibly proud of you. You've been the true definition of a survivor, and now you've taken on the role of helping others see the light at the end of their tunnel. You've filled the gap of being more than a big brother but also my father, best friend, and bishop. You're the true definition of a servant, selfless leader. You've been there through the best and the worst of my years. I've faced challenges I couldn't understand, but you've been by my side, helping me understand that God's love is greater than any other. When I was weak mentally and emotionally, you helped me renew my strength through God's teachings. Congratulations! We're all so proud of you.

Love,
Baby Sister PetaGaye Lee-Agyemang

Chapter 1

The Spirit of Abortion

Don't abort your purpose!

[11] For I know the plans and thoughts that I have for you,' says the LORD, 'plans for peace and well-being and not for disaster to give you a future and a hope. **Jer. 29:11 (AMP)**

[15] But when He, Who had chosen and set me apart [even] before I was born and had called me by His grace (His undeserved favor and blessing), saw fit and was pleased. [16] To reveal (unveil, disclose) His Son within me so that I might proclaim Him among the Gentiles (the non-Jewish world) as the glad tidings (Gospel), immediately I did not confer with flesh and blood [did not consult or counsel with any frail human being or communicate with anyone. **Galatians 1:15-16 AMPC**

Have you ever wondered why you always start something and never seem to be able to complete it? You started your education, but you dropped out of school; you start college, and you drop out after only 1 semester; you start a job and before you get a promotion you allow the things that's going wrong, to force you to quit; you start a relationship and before it could fully develop into something great and rewarding like marriage, you quit... Well, if that's you and you can identify with at least one of these issues and for some of us we may be able to relate to all of them like I was. Then sit back, relax, grab a cup of coffee or tea and let's go on this journey together.

In order to deal with an issue and overcome that issue we have to first identify and face that issue itself. We must ask ourselves this question... What are the spirits working behind the scenes of our life, that is causing the breakdown in our progress in life keeping us from achieving our goals. We all have goals, dreams, and aspirations in life to be the best, to achieve success and to establish a loving family. For some of us we face the spirit of **Fear**... We either deal with the fear of failure or to be honest, some face the fear of success.

Why are we fearful of doing what it takes to achieve our goal? The answer quite simply is that most of us have become so comfortable in the state that we are in that we don't have the courage nor the boldness to take the risk of moving to that next level. Some have not developed the soundness of mind to overcome the challenges and be Intentional about succeeding in life. Paul reminds us in the book of-

2 Timothy 1:7 - [7] For God has not given us a spirit of fear, but of power and of love and of a sound mind.

As individuals once we have become comfortable with a certain level in life we settle for that level and as a result, we at times settle for mediocrity: the mediocre job, the mediocre relationship, and the mediocre spiritual level in God, simply because we have become comfortable in that state. But if you are tired of settling for the "just enough" and you want to ascend to the level of more than enough and the greater that God has for you in your career, business, relationship and ministry then we must first conquer the fear of the unknown. The next level is unknown to us and what we are afraid of is stepping into that unknown. In order to get what you have never had; you have to do something you've never done.

Conquer fear!

Nelson Mandela once said "I learned that courage was not the absence of fear, but the triumph over it. The brave man is not he who does not feel afraid, but he who conquers that fear."

There's a spirit working behind all of this, and it's called the spirit of Abortion...

The term "spirit of abortion" is a metaphorical idea of "aborting our purpose in life"; it might involve feelings of giving up on goals or aspirations. Aborting one's purpose in life can have profound effects on various aspects of an individual's well-being.

On a personal level, it may lead to a sense of emptiness and lack of fulfillment. Without a clear sense of purpose, individuals might struggle to find meaning in their daily activities, resulting in a diminished quality of life.

Moreover, the impact extends to mental health. A purpose serves as a motivating force, providing a sense of direction and goals. When one abandons or neglects their purpose, it can contribute to feelings of anxiety, depression, and a general sense of aimlessness. Mental well-being is closely tied to having a purpose, and its absence can significantly impact emotional resilience.

This spirit you may ask, where does it come from, how did I end up with this spirit, and how do I get rid of it?

Well, if you were to take the time to gain clarity and an understanding of spiritual things, you will begin to understand that the spirit came upon you before birth from a thought or an act. Our thoughts formulate our actions and as we think about a thing, there are spirits that are released behind that thought. Understanding the law of Attraction and how the spiritual world operates, I've come to the understanding that whatever words or thoughts you release into the atmosphere is the same spirit you will attract.

Proverbs 18:21 [21] Death and life are in the power of the tongue: and they that love it shall eat the fruit thereof.

Mark 11:22-24 "[22] So Jesus answered and said to them, "Have faith in God. [23] For assuredly, I say to you, whoever says to this mountain, 'Be removed and be cast into the sea,' and does not doubt in his heart, but believes that those things he says will be done, he will have whatever he says. [24] Therefore I say to you, whatever things you ask when you pray, believe that you receive *them,* and you will have *them.*

For many of us our mothers during and after the pregnancy may have been dealing with various concerns and issues surrounding the pregnancy. These issues may have mainly been emotional discord. This emotional distress or discord may have arisen from her becoming pregnant at an early age, thus causing a "thought" of having an abortion. Abortion may have been considered as an option because the pregnancy may have been viewed as a mistake, not receiving support from the father - meaning him expressing his opinion of not wanting the child or perhaps the thought of the pressure or possibly being a single mother. So many possible odds against the woman and her pregnancy including the negative opinions of others and the urging and suggestion from others to abort the child. Some may have gone as far as offering to pay and making a suggestion of where to go to have the abortion. Which was the case for my mother, and through that advice given it formulated a thought; that spirit was created. The thought of abortion entered my mother's mind, and she "thought" about doing it, but it never happened so as a result the spirit of abortion was placed on my life. This is not a figment of imagination my friends this is something real. This was my life; this is my story.

The Act of Conception

When I was conceived in my mother's womb, she now was open to having to face many pressures of life. This was brought on immediately because of my father denying paternity and expressing the unborn child (me) was not his. She was also a teenager living with her parents and would now have to face her mother as an unwed, pregnant teen girl. Culturally where I am from in the Island of Jamaica this was not accepted traditionally and was frowned upon. Being a teenage girl in this predicament, she was seen as a failure. This now placed my mother in a very uncertain stage in life and the questions of how I move forward; how do I face my mother; how will I be viewed in the community as a 15-year-old being with child? What would now become of my life, my future, my goals? The enemy saw this as an opportunity and he now plants the seed of abortion in her mind and to convince her even more to agree with the thought of abortion, she had someone close to her encouraging her and suggesting a place to go to have the abortion, made the thought even more real.

Nothing just happens, before your mother met your father before the very foundation of the earth was formed God had a purpose and God had a plan for your life, but the enemy also has a purpose, and he has a plan. John 10:10 states, "the thief cometh not, but for to steal, and to kill, and to destroy"; but the scripture did not stop there because God always have a final say in the situation. The scripture continues, "But I (God) am come that they might have life, and that they might have it more abundantly."

The enemy wants you to be conquered by this spirit of abortion, so you'll never become who God has intended for you to become, but God has a plan for you to be more than a Conqueror: **Romans 8:37** "Nay, in all these things we are more than conquerors through him that loved us". In order to get pass the fear factor we have to know what the word of God says about us, and what does God say regarding that fear, and doubt, he said again in **2 Timothy 1:7 AMP** [7] "For God did not give us a spirit of timidity or cowardice or fear, but [*He has given us a spirit*] of power and of love and of sound judgment and personal discipline [*abilities that result in a calm, well-balanced mind and self-control*]."

See the enemy wants us to have thoughts of Doubt and Fear because that's his thing and what he works with, but our God on the other hand wants us to Believe in Him and wants us to have Faith. Without Faith as the scripture says in Hebrews 11:6, "It's impossible to please God without Faith, because as long as we come to him with our hopes and future desires, we must then Believe that He is a Rewarder of those who diligently seek him."

So, with that in mind, what's stopping you from believing, what's stopping you from dreaming, what's stopping you from acting. Get up from that place of setback and press your way knowing that God is able... All God is waiting for you to do is just ask him or better yet imagine it... Imagine yourself being a Millionaire, Imagine yourself being a Real Estate owner, Imagine yourself not just buying a car from the dealership but Owning the dealership; imagine yourself being that Pastor, Evangelist, Prophet, Apostle or Teacher He has called you to be... Being that world changer, yes you who thought it was over, yes you who thought you were not worthy enough, yes you who have already aborted several things… Here's what the word says to help you with that request or thought…

Ephesians 3:20 (AMP) [20] "Now to Him who is able to [carry out His purpose and] do superabundantly more than all that we dare ask or think [*infinitely beyond our greatest prayers, hopes, or dreams*], according to His power that is at work within us".

I decree over you that you are now Empowered to Win, Empowered to Conquer, Empowered to GO FORTH!!! I encourage you today that your dream is not dead Joseph, the Plot can't stop you, the Pit can't hold you, the Prison can't contain you and the spirit of Abortion can no longer hold you back. It's your TIME, it's your SEASON, the tides have shifted, and the clouds are gone, darkness has an expiration; and it expires now!!!

Isaiah 60:1-2 (AMP) [1]"Arise [*from spiritual depression to a new life*], shine [*be radiant with the glory and brilliance of the Lord*]; for your light has come, And the glory and brilliance of the Lord has risen upon you. [2] "For in fact, darkness will cover the earth and deep darkness will cover the peoples; But the Lord will rise upon you [*Jerusalem*] And His glory and brilliance will be seen on you.

Throughout my life everything that I set out to do, I would get to a certain point of completion and then an overwhelming spirit would come over me and have me believe I couldn't complete, finish or accomplish that task. That spirit would have me believe what I was attempting to complete was impossible, especially since I had no support or resources to see it through. And because of this belief, I'd suddenly give up, quit, and abort whatever I was trying to complete or accomplish. Is there anyone out there who can relate to what I've experienced. Some of you reading this book right now may have either been through it, still going through it, or will eventually face it.

I was able through the skills of playing Soccer, which was my passion and dream, to obtain a Full Scholarship to one of the top High Schools in the Island of Jamaica, St. Jago High School in the Parish (State) of St. Catherine in the City of Spanish Town. I was doing well when I started, I was recognized in my class as a top student and was given many roles. The moment I started to excel, the spirit came in and I aborted my passion and drive to learn and started to fall behind. I made it through High school primarily on my athletic skills and not academics.

I graduated High School at almost the lowest class they had; I started out well but aborted my academic abilities to excel.

I migrated to the USA in 1995 and was living in Teaneck, New Jersey with my grandmother, mother and two sisters. I started college courses at Bergen Community College and was excited about continuing my education but after one full semester I dropped out; the spirit of abortion was at work again. This spirit continued to haunt me for many, many years, and many things I started I ended up giving up, terminating, or aborting.

I was in a service one day and I heard my Spiritual father the Late Apostle Devon A Swaby, speaking about a spirit called abortion. He spoke of it in such a profound way. I remember him saying if you've been dealing with these signs and events in your life, check back and see if your mother thought of or attempted to abort you while you were in her womb. Well, I left that service and not long after that I called my mother and inquired; she was reluctant to tell me, but I reassured her it was for my good to know.

As my mother told me the story she started to cry. I thanked my mother for telling me the full story because I understood 95% of deliverance (being delivered from a thing), is first **Identification**. You cannot deliver or be delivered from what you don't identify. That's why when you visit a doctor you are given a lengthy questionnaire, or they verbally ask you a ton of questions; they do this to identify the source of the issue in order to then prescribe the right treatment for the issue. My issue required a Spiritual Treatment and that night I stood in the power of the Holy Spirit and my mother, and I went through Spiritual Deliverance, and I prayed against the Spirit of Abortion. Next, my mother repented of the thought and commanded that spirit to leave.

I was able to finally overcome that spirit of abortion and did not abort what God has purposed in my life and on 09/13/2015 my wife and I were able to give birth to our ministry Empowered To Win International Ministries and have experience the Favor and Glory of God in the ministry. I was able to now move forward and fully complete whatever tasks or goals I had in life. I have since been able to travel to so many countries such as Germany to speak into the lives of others and share the good news of Salvation. I survived that spirit and gave birth and so can you. I decree the breakers anointing on your life today and every yoke of spiritual abortion, every burden of the oppressor must be broken today according to:

Isaiah 10:27 (NKJV) [27] It shall come to pass in that day That his burden will be taken away from your shoulder, And his yoke from your neck, And the yoke will be destroyed because of the anointing oil.

Pray this prayer and confessions with me today!

"The Lord will perfect that which concerneth me: thy mercy O Lord, endureth forever: forsake not the works of thine own hands." **Psalm 138:8**:

"Lift up your heads, O ye gates; and be ye lift up, ye everlasting doors; and the King of glory shall come in." **Psalm 24:7**

Now let's confess!

1. I confess my sins of exhibiting occasional doubts.
2. Let the angels of the living God roll away the stone blocking my financial, physical, and spiritual breakthroughs, in Jesus' name.
3. I bind every spirit manipulating my beneficiaries against me, in the name of Jesus.
4. I remove my name from the book of seers of goodness without manifestation, in the name of Jesus.
5. Let God arise and let all the enemies of my breakthrough be scattered, in the name of Jesus.
6. Let the fire of God melt away the stones hindering my blessings, in the mighty name of Jesus.
7. Let the cloud blocking the sunlight of my glory and breakthrough be dispersed, in the name of Jesus.
8. All secrets of the enemy in the camp of my life that are still in the darkness, let them be revealed to me now, in Jesus' name.
9. All evil spirits planning to trouble me, be bound, in Jesus' name.

10. Lord, let me not put unprofitable and heavy loads upon myself, in the name of Jesus.
11. All keys to my goodness that are still in the possession of the enemy, Lord, give them unto me.
12. Open my eyes, O Lord, and let not my ways be darkened before me.
13. All my sweat on the affairs of my life will not be in vain, in the name of Jesus.
14. The pregnancy of good things within me will be not be aborted by any contrary power, in the name of Jesus.
15. Lord, turn me to untouchable coals of fire.
16. Lord, let wonderful changes begin to be my lot from this week.
17. Lord, remove covetousness from my eyes.
18. Lord, fill the cup of my life to the brim.
19. Let every power stepping on my goodness receive God's arrow of fire now, in the name of Jesus.
20. I reject every spirit of the tail in all areas of my life, in Jesus' name.
21. I repent of the thought of abortion from my mother, and I destroy that spirit of abortion operating in my life by the fire of God in the mighty name of Jesus.
22. Thank God for the victory.

Chapter 2

The Spirit of Rejection

You're not a Mistake, God has always known you and accepted you as His own...

According to **Merriam-Webster Dictionary**, the word rejection means the action of rejecting; the state of being rejected. Rejection occurs when a person or group of people excludes an individual and refuses to acknowledge or accept them. Abandonment is a similar term, meaning to desert someone, to leave and never return. Rejection takes many forms. It may occur through the ending of a relationship, someone losing a job, or through criticism. Feelings of rejection also can arise from abandonment by friends or family or close relations such as a parent or a spouse.

Reactions to rejection may include disappointment, anger, sadness, depression, and abandonment. Rejection may cause you to stop trying because of fear of rejection.

You Are Not Alone in Your Rejection

Many people in the Bible experienced rejection. The Old Testament prophets were often rejected and disrespected. They ended up in lion's dens, pits, and were martyred. Joseph whose story is recorded in Genesis, was rejected by his family and his brothers sold him into slavery. Moses experienced repeated rejection before Pharaoh.

In the New Testament, the Apostle Paul was stoned by a crowd of people, run out of town, and escaped with his life by being let over a wall in a basket. Peter and John were imprisoned, and Stephen experienced the ultimate rejection...he was martyred after preaching one of his greatest messages ever recorded in the New Testament. Everyone experiences rejection. It is impossible to go through life without feeling rejected at some point and time.

God experienced rejection. In Numbers 14:11 the Lord asked Moses: *"How long will these people reject me? How long will they not believe me, with all the signs which I have performed among them?"* **(Numbers 14:11, NKJ)**

Jesus experienced rejection. The prophet Isaiah said concerning Jesus: *"He was despised and rejected by men, a man of sorrows, and familiar with suffering. Like one from whom men hide their faces he was despised, and we esteemed him not,"* (Isaiah 53:3). Jesus came to His own people, and they rejected him (John 1:11) and He was rejected in his own hometown (Mark 6:4). Like Jesus, you will be rejected because you are not of this world, (John 15:18-19).

Ephesians 1:5-6 [5] having predestined us to adoption as sons by Jesus Christ to Himself, according to the good pleasure of His will, [6] to the praise of the glory of His grace, by which He [a]made us accepted in the Beloved.

Jeremiah 1:5 [5]Before I formed you in the womb I knew you [and approved of you as My chosen instrument], And before you were born, I consecrated you [to Myself as My own]; I have appointed you as a prophet to the nations."

There is a joy a mother feels when she sees the face of that wonderful child she has carried for months. There is a joy that child feels when finally, they get to feel that first slap and make that first noise and experience taking that first gasp of breath that life gives. There is the joy of a mother's embrace and feeling loved and cared for as that child grows and goes through the stages of development anticipating what lies ahead from the ones who were chosen to participate in bringing them into the world.

I remember on my twenty-first birthday my wife Paula Davis-Smith threw a surprise birthday party for me and when I had to blow out the candle, my wish was for a son. On 9/16/1997 that same year our first child, a son, Wayne Anthony Smith Jr was born. The joy we felt in that room that day and the look on his face that said, "I now trust you to guide me through life" was unexplainable. Knowing what I went through in my life with my father not being there I made a commitment that I would always be there for him no matter what.

For many like me in the past that joy sadly gets overshadowed by discovering a reality, a reality that no child would ever want to discover. That discovery of realizing that the joy your life was meant to bring is overshadowed by the fact your father was never present, nor accepted you and or discovering your mother gave you up for adoption and now your entire world and life has been affected.

REJECTION has now taken over, there's now a deep empty void you now go through life trying to fill. The more you try, the deeper the void gets; the more hurt you experience, the more you lack confidence and the more you search for acceptance.

This was my life, my story, and this is how it all happened!

Growing up in Jamaica in a home that consisted of a mother, sisters, grandmother, and great-grandma I realized that someone or something was missing... where was my father? I would soon find out that my father already had a family and had other kids, it's a reality I would have to accept and live with for the rest of my life. I was never born into the loving and warm embrace of a proud happy father and mother but only in the arms of a scared and afraid 16-year-old first time mother.

As I began to grow and go through the stages of life from infancy to a toddler to a young innocent child running around, I was able to cope with this reality for a while. Once I had knowledge of who my siblings were and where they lived, which by the way was not far from where I lived, I was excited. I would always find myself going by their home hanging out with my sisters and brothers but never felt that love that a son needs from a father. I was always, "the outside child, the child of a mistake" according to my father.

As I grew older and going through school, the school system in Jamaica did not provide free lunch or lunch programs you had to have money to buy lunch. I remember there were times when I would go to my dad and ask for lunch money only to be told he does not have any. There were times I would get support from him that could barely scratch the surface.

What he gave me could only get me through that day, I used to ask myself the question; my dad is a taxicab driver and he's driving and picking up and dropping off passengers all day and out of the entire week all he could provide me with is one days' worth of lunch money. I could not understand, it just did not make sense, this should not be, I recalled myself saying to myself.

No matter the lack of support, I would always still have a deep love for my father and siblings. But then the older I got, and the more life came at me and demanded from me, the more the rejection came.

I had to learn from an early age how to be an entrepreneur. I began going to the market, buying small chickens and raising them. I was going through the process of preparing them to make Jerk chicken meals and selling the meals on Fridays near my grandfather's business in order to get by and have money for lunch.

I was only nine or ten years old this should not be so. Where's my father, the one who should be the provider, the breadwinner? He was absent; I should not have been born in his eyes and I was a mistake, I was rejected.

I began developing a love and passion for soccer, we call it Football in the Islands of the Caribbean. I ended up falling in love with the position of Goalkeeper. I soon found out my dad played the same position but going through days of training and preparation and seeing other players dads sit and watch them, and then take them home after training made me sad because I had to walk for miles.

I walked for miles for a long time until I was able to get a bicycle. I began riding my bicycle home through the dangerous streets of the community where my school was, and even through my community which was filled with guns and violence and murders.

My dad was a Taxicab driver. I would have games after games and would look to see my dad, but he was never there. The void got deeper and deeper, the absence got louder and louder, the voice sounded stronger and stronger; "*You're Rejected, no one loves you no one cares*".

As mentioned before, because of my skill in soccer, I was offered a Scholarship to attend one of the best schools in the island, St. Jago High. The joy and excitement I felt and in preparation for high school I went to my dad and asked for his support in getting school supplies for school only to be told to go ask my grandmother who was now living in the USA.... *REJECTION.*

I remember he would teach my other brothers how to drive and yet he would never ask me or offer to teach me how to drive his vehicle. Years went by, and I was doing well in Soccer, but my schoolwork was suffering because my passion was driven more for the game of Soccer, girls, friends and popularity, but not for my schoolwork.

As a result of this I failed my exams and was now setback in school. I never had that father to guide me and teach me the principles and disciplines of life needed to survive and achieve your goals. I should have achieved my goals academically in order to remain on track to exit High School after graduation in 1994, but I ended up having to stay back a year to achieve success in my subjects.

Then came Graduation time, a very proud moment, in spite of failing in many things I was still able to make it to graduation, my mom was there with me, but where was dad, he was never there...

As time went by and I grew up achieving many things athletically but not academically, the news came that my grandmother has applied for my mom, sisters, Kennie-Ann and Peta-Gaye and I to migrate to the USA. With this feeling of joy and excitement, I now had to prepare and get my passport. I remember going to my dad and sharing the good news and asking if he would financially cover the cost of helping me in obtaining my passport. He told me, "Ok see me at such and such a time and I'll give you something". The joy I felt at the pinnacle of my life having the opportunity to leave Jamaica a place where we were poor and struggling, finally to go to America a land filled with so much potential.

I remember waiting and waiting and waiting and back then there were no cell phones or pay phones for me to use to call my dad, so I had to wait until it got dark because where I thought he would meet me he changed his route and I had to take the long journey back home empty hurt and rejected.

He then said to meet him there another time, and I went and waited, and waited, he never showed up. I also remember one day when I got to the bus station, and I finally saw him and as I got closer, he pulled off and I ran after the car but was left looking at the rear end of the vehicle. Empty hurt and rejected...

I finally met him and when I asked him about the support he promised, he advised me once again, "Go ask your grandmother she's abroad in the USA". Again, I was left empty, hurt, and rejected...

Before I migrated to the USA in early 1995, I was able to fulfil a long-hoped-for dream that my best friend Mark Thomas and I dreamt of when we were only boys growing up, to make it to the Pro's in Soccer and play under the National Stadium lights. My dream had come to fruition, and I was drafted on my final season in high school to play Professional Soccer for a championship contending team.

As I looked in the stands in hopes of seeing my dad, he was never there. I had given my life to the Lord when I was only 13 years old and I was given a Prophetic word from my Spiritual Father Bishop Rowan Edwards (more to come about him), and after getting saved I still struggled to be faithful and committed to the church. I was always looking for acceptance and security and found that in the streets and in females.

The Migration...

I migrated to USA in 1995 and as I got adjusted and settled in, I found myself hanging out with the wrong crowd, I started smoking and drinking but soon realized that my spirit man was fighting against what the flesh wanted to do. I finally gave up and got back in the church.

The more I went and served, the more my passion for God grew. As I grew and matured in God and I developed an intimate relationship with Him, I heard His voice clearly and He spoke to me and said I should start going to a Bible School.

I got excited and went to my Pastor and told him what the Lord had said to me and like a kid filled with excitement and hope expecting to hear something positive, only to be told, "Go sit down you're not ready for that yet" (*Rejection*). I was now 19 years old trapped in a traditional church body that did not know how to support their youth into their purpose, all I could think about was here I go again, facing rejection.

Experiencing rejection from a natural father who was never there to believe and support me now to have a spiritual father to reject me, it doesn't get any worse than this.... My confidence was shattered, my hopes and dreams of that next level of what I was experiencing, was all now gone because of that spirit again, Rejection.

The Migration continued and now the Lord showed me a Vision and told me when I see this sign, I will know this is the place... In the midst of all the rejection the one thing that remained was my Passion and Intimate relationship with God that I had discovered and held on dearly to the scripture found in

Psalm 27:10 (AMP) [10] Although my father and my mother have abandoned me, Yet the LORD will take me up [adopt me as His child.

The Lord had confirmed the vision he showed me when I came to visit Georgia, and my family and I relocated to Georgia in 2002 and we started attending a ministry and after years of commitment, I experienced the same thing again. *Rejection!!!*

All these occurrences of Rejection began to grow branches of Oppression, Depression, and thoughts of Suicide. The branch of suicide now began to grow and at the age of 13, that branch almost bore fruit; "I Almost Did It".

Chapter 3

I Almost Did It

"Cursed be the day I was born! May the day my mother bore me not be blessed! ¹⁵ Cursed be the man who brought my father the news, who made him very glad, saying, "A child is born to you—a son!" ¹⁶ May that man be like the towns the LORD overthrew without pity. May he hear wailing in the morning, a battle cry at noon. ¹⁷ For he did not kill me in the womb, with my mother as my grave, her womb enlarged forever. ¹⁸ Why did I ever come out of the womb to see trouble and sorrow and to end my days in shame? - **Jeremiah 20:14-18**

Have you ever been to a place where you question your very existence, 'why was I even born, why am I here, does anyone love me'? Well, I was there, and it was a very empty lonely feeling. After the enemy could not destroy me from the womb, nor when I was born, the rejections that I went through, started to weigh me down. I felt I was all alone. I felt that no one cared, and I felt like the only person who was there, my mother, had turned her back on me.

The First Time

So, after growing up struggling with the fact that my dad was not there, I was an outside child missing out on the joys and pleasures of family time with mom, dad, and other siblings. For me that was only a fantasy, it was never my reality. My mother, Petal, was a hard-working woman, always trying to do all she could so that we could have food on the table, a roof above our head and clothes to wear. It was never easy for her; because she was young herself and had a child while she was a teenager. Not knowing how to properly balance everything, my grandmother, Esmie, played an important role in my life, but she then migrated to the USA. After my grandmother migrated that put another dent into my already frail and fragile circle of support. Though her migration would present an opportunity for her to support us while overseas, it would still take time for her to settle and get herself established.

Struggling to find my identity and navigate my way through the early stages of life, I could have gone in many different directions, but I decided to surrender my life to the Lord at the age of 13. After that, I had the support of a church family but there was still something missing, there was that Mentor, that Father Figure, that Role Model. I was at a very vulnerable place of acceptance; my uncle then moved into our home for a short period and things got worst.

Having my mother and the only person that I know loves and supports me was everything to me, but when my uncle moved in and started to have his friends over after school leaving a mess in the kitchen, when my mom got home, I would be the one who would be disciplined for it and when you have a Jamaican parent who disciplines you, it's something you remember for life.

Everything started to go downhill. I was already suffering from rejection from my father, my grandmother had migrated to the United States, my mother was struggling to provide and support us, things that I dreamed of seemed a lost cause, and now to make matters worse, the only person I thought loved and cared for me was disciplining me for someone else's wrongdoing.

As I sat in my room one evening, alone, afraid, discouraged, rejected, and hopeless, I heard a voice speaking in my head telling me that *I'm nothing, I'm worthless and rejected, that no one loves or cares for me and that there's no need to exist anymore,* so, the next best thing to do is to end my life because no one will even miss me.

I started to feel like this was the only way out because this sounded true. As I walked the lonely road between the Spanish Town Hospital and my community, I was led to the back of the community where there was a bridge called the "Rio Cobri Bridge".

On my way there I saw some of my church brothers and sisters hanging out and I felt like going over to be with them but the voice speaking lies to me in my head was very convincing that the only way out was to just end my life. The fruit of suicide was getting ready to bear, and this was my way out and I kept on walking.

I got to the bridge and fear, hurt, pain and the Rejection overtook me as I began reflecting on everything. I looked over the railing of the bridge and saw nothing but rocks and a little flow of water and thought to myself, "Surely this will be quick because by the time I fall from this high I would die on impact on the rocks below". I sat there and waited because vehicles were coming, and I thought to myself if someone see's that I'm sitting on the edge to jump over they would try to stop me. I sat there and waited until the vehicles would go by and then there were no vehicles in sight and the moment I believed had finally arrived. With tears flowing from my eyes and the empty feeling I had, I decided that it was time. I sat on the edge and put both feet over the railings and had finally got to the place of, "It is finished, this meaningless, rejected life is finished".

Someone may be reading this book who can relate to this place that I was at, where you felt like there was no hope, all is lost, no one cares about you, your life is meaningless and that nothing matters to me anymore, all that's left is to end it all. The tears flowing, the hurt and pain, the feeling of emptiness, why am I here, why do I even exist, why was I brought into this world to suffer like this?

All the 'why's' started to run through my head, all the while I kept hearing, *"Jump, Just Jump, Just Do It"*. The moment had finally come the opportunity was now here, there was surely no turning back, I'd arrived at this point because of all that I've already gone through, experienced and suffered only being on this earth for 13 years.

No kid should have to suffer like this, be rejected and backed into a dark place like this. I couldn't see the light of day, darkness and dark thoughts had overtaken me, my mind was made up, I was almost aborted so now I'm fighting against a spirit of abortion to abort my very only life.

I was *rejected* by my father and now I was struggling with the spirit of rejection, suffering with my identity, suffering with failure; I had one option and one option only at this point and it was just to do it, to jump, to end it all. It was at this very moment that I would get understanding on a personal level at a very early age the meaning of the scripture below:

Psalm 118:17 AMPC [17] I shall not die but live and shall declare the works and recount the illustrious acts of the Lord.

Death was at my door; death was the way out of this dark place that I was in. Not only was I experiencing dark thoughts, dark experiences, dark moments in my life, but the bridge that I was on, sitting on the railings, I was literally in darkness because there were no lights on the bridge, no cars approaching and so at that very moment it was an indication that this was my life, my moment, my destiny.

This was the moment... just jump! But then, something happened, something that would change my destiny, something that would take away all those hurts and pains that I had felt for all these years. There's a saying that goes "There's a light at the end of the Tunnel".

A light at the end of the tunnel is an idiomatic expression because we use its figurative meaning over the literal one. This phrase refers to an object, person (Me), or situation (Mine) that gives someone a reason to believe that a bad situation is ending.

Seeing the lights at the end of a tunnel means you have seen something or someone that gives you some kind of hope for the future after a long time of experiencing difficulties. It is a good sign that something beautiful is happening.

Origin

The phrase comes from the idea of being in a pitch-black tunnel and suddenly seeing your way out to a beautiful destination. The common phrase dates back at least to the 1880s, from what I can tell. It was popularized by President John Kennedy in the mid-1960s, referencing the Vietnam war.

Since the phrase light at the end of the tunnel means something or someone that gives hope, here are some words and phrases related to the idiom.

- Hope
- Belief
- Faith
- Confidence

- Hopefulness
- Reassurance
- Conviction
- Trust
- Assurance
- Certainty
- Optimism
- Guarantee
- Positiveness
- Doubtlessness
- Prayer
- Assuredness
- Satisfaction
- Entrustment
- Freedom from suspicion
- Freedom from doubt
- Security
- Comfort
- Acceptance
- Encouragement

Do you think you are a failure because you have failed repeatedly? FAIL means:

- **FIRST**
- **ACTION**
- **IN**
- **LEARNING**

Did you lose everything you have labored hard for many years to gather? Do you feel like taking your life or harming yourself is the ultimate solution?

Moses, Elijah, and Job overcame suicidal thoughts, and depression and they went down in history as some of the greatest men. After his depression and sorrow, Jesus conquered death to give you ultimate victory over the world.

Whatever negative woes of life is fighting you, I want you to know Jesus has already won that battle for you. Your Savior is the Greatest! Your Savior is the ultimate positive ever-present solution. Don't listen to those voices in your head that tell you that you should just take your own life because you will never win the battle against the negatives of life.

Don't listen to those voices that tell you that you have lost the battle. They lied! Listen to Jesus— the voice of truth. Don't let depression and suicidal thoughts win. Run to the Mercy Seat where Jesus is calling. You can't do it on your own, let Jesus help you.

I was on the edge of the bridge, I was at the end, the moment was right, the time was now, and the end was here, BUT I looked up to the skies above, and I saw a Light.

My Prayer for You

1 Peter 5:7, casting all your anxieties on him, because he cares for you. Lord, I pray for anyone, anywhere suffering from depression right now.

In Jesus mighty name, I pull you out of that sink hole of depression, despair and suicide.

Ezekiel 16:6, I passed by you and saw you lying in your blood, and I said to you as you lay in your blood: Live! Yes, I said to you as you lay in your blood: Live!

I come against the spirit of suicide, I come against that lying voice of the devil. In Jesus mighty name Child of God it's not over yet, there's hope for your future. I speak life over you in Jesus mighty name. You shall not die but live to excel and do great exploits.

Stay my brother, my sister, your generation is yet to celebrate you. Your generation is still waiting to hear from you God is not done with you yet Live and not die, in Jesus mighty name

I come against the spirit of depression and despair in you, I come against the spirit of confusion and dejection in you, I come against every form of anxiety attack on you right now, I come against the spirit fear in you right now, in Jesus's name, I come against the spirit of shame on you right now, in Jesus' name, I come against the spirit of guilt on you right now, I come against the spirit of frustration on you right now, I come against anything that has taken away your peace and tranquility, in Jesus mighty name.

I pray you find God's peace that passes all human understanding today in Jesus mighty name. I pray that the hands of the Lord lift you up and out of, that pit of depression and despair, in Jesus mighty name. I pray that whatever is responsible for your pain, be destroyed now in Jesus mighty name. I pray that, that pain you're carrying, be it emotional, medical, relational, financial even marital. May the Lord send help your way. I pray for divine intervention for you today in Jesus mighty name.

I pray the sun and the Son of righteousness will rise with healing on His wings over you, and drip you with heavenly medicines of comfort, peace and restoration, even now in Jesus mighty name.

May the sweet presence of the Holy Spirit overshadow you right now in Jesus mighty name. **Psalms 42:11** - Why am I so depressed? Why is this turmoil within me? Put your hope in God, for I will still praise Him, my Savior and my God. I pray the Lord send the right people your way, that will offer you the help you need, in Jesus mighty name. Be encouraged child of God even this shall pass.

Keep your hope alive. Help is on the way

Chapter 4

I saw a Light (Darkness has an Expiration) ...

¹Arise [from the depression and prostration in which circumstances have kept you—rise to a new life]! Shine (be radiant with the glory of the Lord), for your light has come, and the glory of the Lord has risen up on you!

² For behold, darkness shall cover the earth, and dense darkness [all] peoples, but the Lord shall arise upon you [O Jerusalem], and His glory shall be seen on you. - **Isaiah 60:1-2 AMPC**

The Apostle Peter declared in the book of:

1 Peter 5:8 Be sober, be vigilant; because your adversary the devil, as a roaring lion, walketh about, seeking whom he may devour.

If you ever wonder why we come under attack on a constant basis as we navigate through life's journey, it is because the devil doesn't rest, the scripture says he goes about like a roaring lion looking for whom to devour. So, if the power of darkness is not at rest day and night, why should you, their target, rest? No wonder the scripture instructed that we pray without ceasing.

The power of darkness are the rulers of the world, powers, and principalities in high places. And if you think they are physical enemies that you can overcome with your physical strength, remember the scripture says by strength shall no man prevail. The book of **Ephesians 6:12** says, "For our struggle is not against flesh and blood, but against the rulers, against the authorities, against the powers of this dark world and against the spiritual forces of evil in the heavenly realms". They are rulers of darkness, immeasurable numbers of unseen spirits terrorizing the lives of people.

There are so many people whose life has been disturbed by the power of darkness; the Lord is about to set you free today. The scripture **John 1:5** "And the light shineth in darkness; and the darkness comprehended it not". The light of God will shine eminently in your life today, and the stronghold of darkness tormenting your life will flee today. There was a very dark light that was shining over my life even though the Omnipotent and Omniscient God knew that I had a brighter future than the darkness I was facing.

Have you ever been walking in broad daylight where the sun is shining, and you can physically see where you're going but at the same time you can't see where you're going because of the darkness that's surrounding you.

You Have Darkness of Oppression

According to Webster's Dictionary.com Oppression Is *the feeling of being heavily burdened, mentally or physically, by troubles, adverse conditions, anxiety, etc.* I was that person that was dealing with the heavy burdens that often come with life challenges, growing up without a father and having to face life on your own is a very difficult task. The majority of things in this life comes with a "How-To" manual but there's not a "How-To" Manual other than the word of God, but even Jesus needed the guidance of the Father:

John 5:19-20 AMPC [19] So Jesus answered them by saying, I assure you, most solemnly I tell you, the Son is able to do nothing of Himself (of His own accord); but He is able to do only what He sees the Father doing, for whatever the Father does is what the Son does in the same way [in

His turn]. [20] The Father dearly loves the Son and discloses to (shows) Him everything that He Himself does. And He will disclose to Him (let Him see) greater things yet than these, so that you may marvel and be full of wonder and astonishment.

Now let's look at the significance of an absent father in a child's life. A child looks to the father for guidance, strength, hope and security. When the father is not there the child is left without a guide and not adequately capable of navigating life and therefore will take on burdens and responsibilities from a very early age, which have led many young men and young women to seek that guidance from the streets and turn to negatively impacting things. This puts them in a state of darkness where they can't see their way out of situations. Jesus said, "the Son is able to do nothing of Himself (of His own accord); but He is able to do only what He sees the Father doing, for whatever the Father does is what the Son does in the same way [in His turn]". That simply means the son needs that guidance because there's a time coming when the son will have to do what he has learned in his turn/time in life. When that turn or time comes and there's nothing you have learned then it leads you into darkness.

But as Isaiah 60 says, *It's Time to Arise.* You must rise and shine, Shine the light of Jesus that's upon your life into the darkness of your life. It says... Arise [from the depression and prostration in which circumstances have kept you—rise to a new life]! Shine [be radiant with the glory of the Lord], for your light has come, and the glory of the Lord has risen up on you!

You must put on your spiritual warfare because we are fighting a spiritual battle. I decree by the authority of heaven that God will crush your enemy to death in the name of Jesus. People are walking in darkness. The life of many people has been characterized by gross darkness; the scripture says in the book of **Isaiah 9:2,** "The people who walk in darkness will see a great light; Those who live in a dark land, The light will shine on them". You will see a great light today; heaven will announce you to your Helper who has not been able to locate you due to the gross darkness upon you.

The enemy of your soul would love for you to isolate and fall into depression during this dark season. Refuse to give in. Don't hide your light. Now is our time to shine for all the world to see.

The god of this age has blinded the mind of those who hear the gospel and reject it. Life is in the gospel, and that light is in us — The entrance of your words gives light...."It gives understanding to the simple"- **Psalm 119:130.**

This explains why the darkness did not comprehend the light. Light cannot penetrate the eyes of a blind person. So, if the enemy can blind you, he will. I was blinded by the enemy of Oppression, Depression, Rejection, Insecurity and Hopelessness.

When we are wise, then the enemy of our soul changes tactics. And no wonder! For Satan himself transforms himself into an Angel of light as stated in **2 Corinthians 11:14,** "For those of us who can see and comprehend the light". The deceiver transforms himself into what appears to be light, but it is not the true light.

John 1:6-9 "There was a man sent from God, whose name was John. This man came for a witness, to bear witness of the Light, that all through Him might believe. He was not that Light but was sent to bear witness of that

Light. That was the true Light which gives light to every man coming into the world."

My life was filled with darkness in the light of all the talents and gifts I had hidden inside of me that could not be seen because of the darkness that surrounded me. I was growing up in a community filled with darkness, I was hanging out with people filled with darkness and I was being raised by men that was filled with darkness.

Your life can be defined by people of authority over you who speak words into your life that you accept, and God did not mean for you in life. That person for me was my teacher, she was the authority figure in my life while I was in school.

There was a very notorious gunman in my country who was labeled with a particular name, he was called Sandocan. He was a well-known murderer who was on the Island's #1 Wanted List. We had the same name, and it came across the radio one day that police had gunned him down and he died.

I was sick and missing from school for two days and it was announced on the radio, but my teachers and classmates did not hear that it was him, but they heard when his real name was mentioned which was the same exact name as mine. They thought it was me and they now feared I was dead.

When I showed up in class everyone was amazed after thinking I was dead but here, I was. I told them it was the wanted gunman that was killed. My teacher turned to me and said something that would then cast a Dark Spell over my life. She said from today I will now call you "Sandocan", the nickname of the deceased gunman.

I was now known in my community and high school by this name and at the age of 19, darkness kicked in. I was at school one day in the pavilion sitting with friends and this guy started to mock and make fun of me. The things he said and the way it made me feel put me into a state of mind of darkness.

In my community the don who ran the area came to me and gave me a gun to keep. At the age of 19, I was now carrying the name of a murderer, I was giving a gun to keep, and I was mocked and made fun of. The dark spirit of Rejection and Depression was surrounding me and the only thought that came to me was to go home, get the gun and kill him. Darkness was now setting in and I wanted him dead.

I went home, got the gun and went back to the campus and went up to the pavilion but he was not there. I was so enraged that if those who remained there had said anything to me, I was determined to kill them. I knew where we all hung out, so I set out to find him there. On my way there I heard the voice of God asking me... *"Is It Worth It?"*

The voice of God spoke and the dark spirit that was over me left and I went home. When you are surrounded by darkness, nothing that represents light matters to you if you are not in the right frame of mind to see the light.

When I was taking that long walk to the bridge at age 13, that spirit speaking darkness into my soul telling me that I'm rejected and no one cares was leading me to, there were not many lights. While I was walking on the road the lights of the vehicles shined on me, which back then if I'd had understanding I would have known and discerned in the spirit realm the Light of God was shining on me in the midst of that dark period. When I got to the point in my journey where I saw my friends gathered at one of their homes, there was a light there and they were standing underneath it and that was the Light of God leading me to them to speak to them so that peradventure they could guide me out of that dark period. But I kept on walking because the darkness of the voice shone brighter than the voice of light that was speaking to me. At that time in my life the place was dark except for the areas where light was. That's how life is, there will be moments in this journey of life where there will be areas that are dark and when they are dark, they seem extremely dark.

Then there will be areas of light but based on the nature of your darkness that you are facing; the light will seem insignificant. Those lights that were shining seemed insignificant to the darkness of rejection and hopelessness I was facing.

The moment was here, the stage was set, the scene was ready to be played out, in a country where many young men and women, old men and women, middle-aged men and women, died from the act of suicide, it was my turn, I was next.

Darkness had taken over, I could no longer see the light of hope to live, and I was ready to follow the darkness to the end, the end of my life, I was ready, I got this far, I sat on the bridge, I looked down at the river below. It's perfect, no water running, rocks everywhere and a big concrete foundation that held up the bridge.

I told myself I would aim for that so that I would die on impact. I was in position, a car was coming, and I repositioned, now the car had passed, that light went by one last time and it was now the opportunity for me to jump.

As I got myself in position to jump, I said to myself, *'don't look down, just look up and jump'*. As I lifted my head up to the skies, I saw a light, it was a light like I'd never seen before, it was a light that caught my attention, it was a light that silenced the voice of Rejection, silenced the voice of Depression, silence the voice of Death and it silenced the voice of Suicide. It was the voice of-

Isaiah 60:1-2 AMPC [1] Arise [*from the depression and prostration in which circumstances have kept you—rise to a new life*]! Shine (*be radiant with the glory of the Lord*), for your light has come, and the glory of the Lord has risen upon you! [2] For behold, darkness shall cover the earth, and dense darkness [all] peoples, but the Lord shall arise upon you [*O Jerusalem*], and His glory shall be seen on you.

It was the voice of light that spoke into the Darkness in the book of **Genesis 1:2-4 NLT** [2] The earth was formless and empty, and darkness covered the deep waters. And the Spirit of God was hovering over the surface of the waters. [3] Then God said, "Let there be light," and there was light. [4] And God saw that the light was good. Then he separated the light from the darkness.

It was the light that shone down on me from heaven above and that light declared that darkness has an expiration date. When true light comes then darkness has to expire, and my darkness expired that night. I looked up, I saw the Light and then the next thing that happened changed my life forever. I Heard His Voice.

Pray With Me

I pray that you will speak a word today that will release life and light out your darkness. They who walk in darkness will comprehend the light today, because the light that proceeds from you will consume the darkness. Open your mouth and the words that you speak shall be spirit and life to the hearer. It is so, and so it is, in Jesus' name — Amen!

Father God, Take charge of my life. Help me step into Your authority and be aware of the wiles of the devil. I ask you to rebuke the evil one away from my life and my family. I plead the blood of Jesus over my family and myself. I ask You to help me move into the breakthroughs that You have planned for me today and out of the darkness that the enemy has planned for me today.

Go before me in my spiritual walk, in my relationships, in my career, and even in my finances according to your word in Isaiah 45:2 that you will go before me and level every mountain and make the crooked path straight In Jesus Name.

Quicken me. Let Your Word give me understanding. Lead me in the way of righteousness that I may understand You better and serve You more effectively. I pray all this in the name of Jesus, Amen.

Chapter 5

I Heard His Voice (Don't do it....)

"I didn't die. I lived! And now I'm telling the world what God did. God tested me, he pushed me hard, but he didn't hand me over to Death. Swing wide the city gates—the righteous gates! I'll walk right through and thank God! This Temple Gate belongs to God, so the victors can enter and praise."- **Psalm 118:17-20 The Message**

Most people want to hear God's voice when they are facing a decision. If only God would speak to us and tell us which choice to make or which direction to embark upon. Many of us claim to have heard God's voice, saying, "God led me to do this," when in fact it was simply our own thoughts and desires that led us in a particular direction.

This is in fact a good way to look at our experiences and the path we take. But there's another side to this. Here's the question I must ask. What if you don't know the voice of God? What if you don't know that it's Him who's speaking to you?

What if you have no experience or encounter to fall back on to say, "Yes, I know this voice and I can trust its direction and instruction? Knowing the voice of God is like knowing your parents, or siblings or even your loved one's voice. This comes overtime from having a consistent and personal relationship with that individual.

You know the voice of your mother because of the relationship that you have established with your mother and therefore if another person's mom comes in the house and calls your name or shouts out instruction or guidance to you, your response will be one of reluctance because you are not familiar with *that* voice and to follow that instruction.

If your mother were to give you the same instruction or guidance you would be quick to follow that instruction and follow what your mom had said because you know that she won't lead you down the wrong path and hearing her voice is one of reassurance.

Hearing a father's voice is even more convincing because a father is more on the side of that Protector. It's the same concept, if you're not familiar with another father's voice you will be reluctant to listen to that voice and you will go down the wrong path.

For me, I was unfamiliar with the voice of God because I had never developed that consistent relationship with him. He speaks to us through His Spirit and if we don't have the Spirit of God dwelling withing us then we cannot respond unless the Spirit connects. That night as I took that long lonely depressing walk from my room to the side of the road in my community on the way to that bridge where I planned to go and jump to end my life, I was hearing voices speaking into my spirit, but I didn't know which one to follow. The word of God declares in - **John 10:10 AMPC** [10] The thief comes only in order to steal and kill and destroy. I came that they may have and enjoy life, and have it in abundance (to the full, till it overflows).

The thief in this instance that I am referring to is the devil, the enemy of our souls. This enemy is the chief deceiver, he's the master deceiver and it was because of deception he was thrown out of heaven.

Revelation 12:9 AMPC [9] And the huge dragon was cast down and out—that age-old serpent, who is called the Devil and Satan, he who is the seducer (*deceiver*) of all humanity the world over; he was forced out and down to the earth, and his angels were flung out along with him.

Definition of Deception- Deception or falsehood is an act or statement that misleads, hides the truth, or promotes a belief, concept, or idea that is not true.

The devil, the deceiver started to point out to me all the reasons why I should do jump, he used the hurt and rejection I was experiencing to hide the truth of **Jeremiah 29:11 NLT** which states, [11] *"For I know the plans I have for you,"* says the Lord. *"They are plans for good and not for disaster, to give you a future and a hope."*

Seeing where my life is now and understanding my purpose now it made sense what the enemy was trying to do but furthermore what God had planned for me. Rejection, especially from a father is one of the most hurtful feelings you can experience in life.

Rejections are the most common emotional wound we sustain in daily life. Whether the rejection we experience is large or small, one thing remains constant — it always hurts, and it usually hurts more than we expect it to.

The question is, why? Why are we so hurt and bothered by not being accepted, why are we so hurt and bothered by not fitting in with the crowd, why are we so hurt and bothered by not having what we see everyone else has that seems like success and security, why?

The answer is — our brains are wired to respond that way. When scientists placed people in functional MRI machines and asked them to recall a recent rejection, they discovered something amazing. The same areas of our brain become activated when we experience rejection as when we experience physical pain. That's why even small rejections hurt more than we think they should, because they elicit literal (albeit, emotional) pain.

"The greatest damage rejection causes are usually self-inflicted. Just when our self-esteem is hurting most, we go and damage it even further."

Of course, emotional pain is only one of the ways rejections impact our well-being. Rejections also damage our mood and our self-esteem, they elicit swells of anger and aggression, and they destabilize our need to "belong." Unfortunately, the greatest damage rejection causes are usually self-inflicted.

My 1st Suicidal Attempt

All of what I was experiencing was now wrapped up in this one lonely night, I heard the voice giving me all the reasons why this was the way, and it made sense. Why not, no one cares, no one loves me, I have nothing, my family is poor, I don't have the love and support of a father who should guide me through life into becoming someone, so why not?

The closer I got to the highway leading to where the bridge was, I started hearing another voice saying '*NO*'. At this point I was convinced that ending it all was the only way for me. I was close to the bridge, and I heard the voice again saying 'NO'. When I got to the bridge and I looked down, formulating the plan as to where I needed to land when I jumped off, I saw a concrete platform and figured that's it by the time I fall and hit that concrete it'll be over. There was a light, it was the light from an oncoming car, I said to myself that I would wait and not allow anything to stop me, peradventure the person come out the car and stop me.

The car went by, it was dark, as dark as the moment I was facing, as dark as my life experiences. I climbed up, sat on the ledge, put both feet over, positioned myself and then I heard the voice much clearer than I heard before. How did I know that voice to trust it?

When I was between the ages of 8-10, I had two dreams. In the first dream I was taken outside of my house and onto the Veranda (like a patio) and the voice said, "Look Up", I looked up in the sky and I saw Brimstones and Fire, I saw planes falling out the sky and I asked what this is, and the voice said, "It's Judgement Day". I couldn't understand it then, but now that I am operating in my Purpose, I know now what God was showing then that I was destined to change lives and save His people who are willing to be saved from Judgement.

The second dream, I was on a bus filled with people that were drinking, smoking, cursing profanities and doing all manner of evil, I had a bible in my hand, and I was preaching to them, but they were rejecting the Word. The bus crashed and turned over and I saw myself standing on the outside of the bus with the same bible in my hand.

The people were crawling out of the bus, one by one, crying to me saying, "Please lead me to Jesus Christ; I asked what this is, and the voice said, "I've called you to save souls, to preach My Word to the nations". It was the voice of God speaking to me.

I was ready to Jump but then I looked up into the sky, and in the stillness of that night, I saw a Light, and then I heard His Voice, the Voice I heard in my dreams, the voice I heard speaking to me as I was taking my journey to the bridge saying, *"Don't do it!"* I then realized, I know this voice, and His Voice said, *"Don't Do It"*.

I sat there on the bridge, and I cried tears because like a loving father telling a son "Don't Worry, I got you", I heard His reassuring voice saying, *"Don't Do It, I Love You, I'm With You and It Will Be Ok"*. The Voice was Peaceful, Reassuring, Convincing and Hopeful. Then I trusted Him, I trusted His Voice.

The 2nd Suicidal Attempt

That second time finding myself facing suicide I was much older in life. I was now married, and my wife and I had relocated from one state to another, we owned our first home and in addition, at this point we'd also had our second child, our miracle baby Abigail A Smith. This second attempt, on that night I barricaded myself in the room with a loaded gun switching it back and forth, putting it to my head and in my mouth trying to determine *how will I do this, how will I end it all?*

Then I heard His voice!!! I heard His Voice through the voice of my daughter. She knew I was in the room, and she tried to get in and could not and she began to cry and said, "Daddy I wanna come in I wanna be with you."

When my daughter said those words... "I wanna be with you", I did not just hear her voice, but I heard the voice of God saying, *"I'm with you"*. The same voice I heard on the bridge I was now hearing it through my daughter this time and it was reassuring at that time as it was before when I heard it.

I opened the door and let her in. God's voice through my daughter that night saved my life because I chose to not only Hear but Listen to His Voice through her small still loving voice calling out to me.

The 3rd Suicidal Attempt

One morning in May of 2014, I got up like I normally do, made my protein shake that I normally drink before going to the gym and work out. I arrived at the gym and was all set to do my workout. I started out with the bench press because that day I was going to work on my chest. I could not lift the normal weight I normally lift; So, I lessened the weight and still could not lift it.

I went all the way down to 25 lbs. and I still could not lift that. A feeling of depression had set over me and I walked out of the gym and sat in my car for a little while. I then drove off and told myself *'just go home today is just not your day'.*

On my way home I started to cry out of nowhere, tears began flowing down my eyes, and I did not know why. Then my mind and emotions and the spirit of lies and darkness started to speak to me. All I kept hearing was that voice of rejection again, the voice of failure. There were areas of my life that were failing, I was not a committed and faithful husband and distraction started to kick in and I was failing.

The enemy started to remind me that I was a failure from conception, he reminded me that I was a failure from birth, he reminded me that I was a failure with my father and now I'm just a failure in life.

I made it home and I felt hopeless again, no one was home; I went upstairs to my room, and I sat on the bed. At this point I heard that voice of suicide again and this time it came stronger. It said *'take six bottles of pills'*, so I took out six bottles of the strongest pills we had in the drawer. Then the voice said, *'get the gun'*, at this point I had a licensed and registered Glock 30, I took it out and laid it on the bed next to the pills and my earphones that I used for working out.

The scene was set, the moment was now, and this was it. Then I heard His voice again, His voice was very clear, the Voice of God spoke over the Voices I was hearing. God said to me, *"Look in your iPad to this same day and date of 2013"*, when I looked, it was the title of the book He gave me, "I Survived and So Can You". I asked Lord why, and He said, *"Take a Picture of this scene, this is the last time you will face this spirit and this scene will be the cover of the book"*. I took the picture and went to work and could not function and I saw two of my friends and one of them who would later become our family friend, Takisha asked, "What's wrong?" and I showed them the picture and they almost lost it.

The primary way that God speaks to us today is through His revealed, written Word. But what do you do when you face the vicissitudes of life, and you don't even understand clearly the Voice of God. When we want to hear God's voice, the Bible is where we should look. Most of the will of God for our lives is already fully revealed in its pages, and it is simply a matter of our obedience to it. All of Scripture is the will of God, but there are a few places in Scripture that specifically use the term *will of God*, which may be especially interesting to a person who wants to hear God's voice:

"I Heard His Voice" typically refers to a personal experience that one has with God through the challenges of life when He reveals Himself to you. "Hearing and Responding to the voice of God" involves recognizing or perceiving His divine guidance and then taking action or responding accordingly.

Hearing the voice of God often involves a combination of inner revelation, inspiration, and sometimes direct communication. For example, in the Christian Bible, there are instances of prophets receiving messages through visions, dreams, or direct verbal communication.

Prophets in the Old Testament who Heard God's Voice and Responded:

- Moses heard God's voice from the burning bush (Exodus 3:4)
- Elijah experienced a "still small voice" (1 Kings 19:12).

New Testament:

- At Jesus' baptism, a voice from heaven said, "This is my beloved Son, with whom I am well pleased" **(Matthew 3:17)**.

We must hear His Voice and respond in a very humble way! When I heard His voice that night on the bridge I responded, when I heard His Voice that night in that room, I responded and when I heard His voice that day on that bed, I responded. When I responded the response then set the stage for the next chapter of my life. I heard His voice again and then I trusted Him.

Prayer Against Any Form Of Rejection

"What shall we then say to these things? If God be for us, who can be against us?"- **Romans 8:31**

"To the praise of the glory of his grace, wherein he hath made us accepted in the beloved"- **Ephesians 1:6.**

- Father, I break the spirit of rejection and completely destroy it, in the me of Jesus.

- Father, I refuse to feel or be rejected because I know that even if the world rejects me, I have a God who loves me and has accepted me in the beloved, in the name of Jesus.
- Father, I see beyond every form of rejection in my life because I know they are working together for my good, in the name of Jesus.
- Father, bring back the real me that the enemy has stolen and remove that which they projected into me that is causing me rejection, in the name of Jesus.
- Father, let my life reject every spirit of rejection, in the name of Jesus.
- Father, by the power in the blood of Jesus, I come out of every satanic prison causing me rejection, in the me of Jesus.
- Father, I break by fire every curse of rejection running in my family line that overshadows my blessings, in the name of Jesus.
- Father, by the blood of Jesus, I cut off every spirit of rejection in my genes, in the name of Jesus.
- Father, let every yoke of collective rejection afflicting my life and destiny break and die, in the name of Jesus.
- Father, every inherited rejection following me about, I shake you off by the power of the resurrection, in the name of Jesus.
- Father, let every spirit of rejection that is older than me but operating in my life release and die, in the name of Jesus.
- Father, every foundation upon which my life has been built, causing me rejection, I receive deliverance by fire, in the mighty name of Jesus.

- Father, by the blood of Jesus, I revoke all evil decree and verdict of rejection made against me and my family, in the name of Jesus.
- Father, let every spirit of rejection and hatred programmed into my blood by the enemy come out and die, in the name of Jesus.
- Father, thou God of Elijah, arise and destroy every voice of rejection and hatred speaking louder than the voice of breakthrough in my life, In the name of Jesus.
- Father, let every mark of rejection working against my life and destiny be consumed by fire, in the name of Jesus.
- Father, every spirit of rejection and hatred I have as a result of the hand that took care of me is consumed by fire, in the name of Jesus.
- Father, by the consuming fire of heaven, I release myself from every curse of the spirit of rejection placed upon me by the enemy, in the name of Jesus.
- Father, every parental rejection caused by the foul spirit of rejection that has put me in perpetual sorrow, break and die, in the name of Jesus.
- Father, by the fire of the holy ghost, I release my life from every evil effect of the words of rejection that are still manifesting in my life, in the name of Jesus.

Chapter 6

Then I Trusted Him

Never Give up He will make a way...

Trusting fully the voice of God when it seems impossible...

⁵ Trust in the Lord with all your heart; do not depend on your own understanding. ⁶ Seek his will in all you do, and he will show you which path to take. - **Proverbs 3:5-6 NLT**

The Bible tells us that even believers struggle with trusting God because life is hard and cruel at times. But we know there is hope and that joy is possible because of the eternal life we have with Christ. Therefore, God wants us to be full of faith and grow in His divine direction, comforted by the Holy Spirit.

There's security, direction, and joy that comes when we fully trust in the Will and Word of God. The scriptures declare in **Psalm 16:11** that, *"You will show me the way of life, granting me the joy of your presence and the pleasures of living with you forever."*

When we trust and surrender to Him, He will grant us access to His presence and once we're in His presence we get direction from Him; *"The steps of a good man are ordered by the Lord: and he delighteth in his way."*- (**Psalm 37:23**) We get joy and pleasure living daily with Him, granting me the joy of your presence and the pleasures of living with you forever.

Trusting God in hopeless situations is easier said than done. *Hope* is that one word has carried me through so much. I've hoped in Christ because I have seen that God can fix anything. He fixed the brokenness in my life. He fixed the broken relationships in my life, He fixed the rejections in my life, He fixed my life.

Trusting God When It Looks Impossible Is Not a New Need!

People have faced impossible situations from the beginning of time. Trusting God when it looks impossible is not a new need. Today we will revisit the Israelites at the end of the Red Sea to understand how to be still and set aside our fear when all hope feels lost.

"But Moses said to the people, "Do not fear! Stand by and see the salvation of the Lord which He will accomplish for you today; for the Egyptians whom you have seen today, you will never see them again forever."- **Exodus 14:13**

God will fight for you. We defined the Hebrew word 'charash': Be still (don't complain or worry about the real enemy in front of you more than you trust God) because God will fight for you.

'Be still' or 'be silent' was said when the Israelites were facing an impossible situation. It really highlights the fact that God works in impossible situations in our lives. He said in **2 Corinthians 12:9** that "His Strength is made Perfect in our Weakness"

The Israelites Knew About the Impossible!

Some things to know about the context of **Exodus 14:13**:

- The Israelites had done nothing wrong.
- God caused this impossible situation.
- Moses was told some of the details, but we don't see him communicate them to the people.
- The Egyptian army was fierce and angry.
- Without God to save them, this was an impossible situation for Israel.

This is a tough situation, but God has gotten Israel out of worse.

The Israelites were asking God to do the impossible. The Egyptian army was close and there was nowhere to hide. There was no way across the Red Sea.

God tells them, "Do not fear; see God save You... be still," and God saved them.

He can save you from your impossible situation today too. Are you believing God for the impossible?

Trust Is Earned When Action Meets Word

Proverbs 3:5 imparts wisdom to its readers: "Trust in the Lord with all your heart and lean not on your own understanding." There is a big difference between trusting in the Lord and trusting other persons or things. Our trust is not in angels or people or rituals or methodologies but in the Lord alone. And, as the writer of the proverb points out, our trust is not in our own understanding.

To trust in the Lord with all our heart, we must wholly rely upon God's promises, wisdom, power, and love to help us in every circumstance. Human understanding is subject to error. God, on the other hand, sees and understands all. He is the One we can lean on and trust. We should trust the Lord with all our heart because human understanding is tainted by sin, limited wisdom, impulsive assumptions, and faulty emotions. We are not always right. **Proverbs 14:12** reminds us of this: "There is a way that seems right to a man, but its end is the way of death" (emphasis added).

Sin taints our understanding and leads us to destruction (**Ephesians 4:17–18**). "Our knowledge is partial and incomplete" (**1 Corinthians 13:9, NLT**). Should we base our understanding on what is partial, sinful, or destructive? Or should we trust in the God who is all-knowing, all-powerful, all-wise, loving, and has good plans to guide, satisfy, and establish us...as its stated in **Isaiah 58:11 NLT,** "The Lord will guide you continually, giving you water when you are dry and restoring your strength. You will be like a well-watered garden, like an ever-flowing spring".

The voice of God in my Spirit that night was very reassuring and gave me hope. I had to make a decision, do I trust His voice that told me He Loves Me and He's with Me and It's Going To Be Ok, or do I trust the deceptive voice telling me all the reason why my life was worth nothing living for because I was rejected abandoned and broken? It was not an easy decision, for some reading this you may be saying "Why would you want to take your life?" Well, unless you have been to a dark deep place of rejection and hurt you will never understand.

I know that someone out there reading this book right now can relate to being in that frame of mind and getting to that place where you felt like it was the end. If you are there or have faced it then I can assure you that because you are reading this book God came through for you and if you are facing it, I can tell you for a surety, "There is Hope in Trusting His Voice". Develop that Trust in God and in His Word and Will for your life and know that He will come through for you because the Spirit of suicide is real just as the word of God is real.

I decided that night that I would trust His Voice and what He had next for me, not knowing what that "next" was, but I felt that it was better than what was and that He would make a way out of no way. I Trusted His Voice and He Saved My Life. I Trusted His Voice and He gave me a new sense of Direction. I Trusted His Voice and He

Ordered my Steps. I Trusted His Voice and He Gave Me a Voice. I Trusted His Voice and His Word Was True (He Came Through). I am alive today to sit here and write my story to tell someone else that may be feeling the same way, suffering from the Spirit of Rejection. He Made a Way When It Seems That There Was No Way...

The next years of my life would be filled with different levels of challenges as I grew in God learning how to trust Him, and not just Him, but trust His process for my life. I felt like I was experiencing an Abraham moment where God said to him leave his country and He would take him to a land of his own. Not knowing where that was and what he would face and who would be with him, he forsook all and trusted His voice. From there we went on to see for those who have read the story of Abraham how he went on to become the Father of Faith; **Romans 4:16**- Therefore, the promise comes by faith, so that it may be by grace and may be guaranteed to all Abraham's offspring--not only to those who are of the law but also to those who are of the faith of Abraham. He is the father of us all.

For the person out there reading this, life may have caved in on you like a building that collapsed after an earthquake or may have swept you away in the rivers of life's struggles like a tsunami that has come in and washed away a city. If that's you don't give up, if that's you, don't quit, if that's you and the enemy is speaking the lies in your ears that there's no hope and you should do it, just end it all, "Don't Do It". Hear and Trust the Voice of God and He will come through for you.

A Prayer for Trusting God in Hard Times

Lord, I thank You that You are the God of the impossible. You can do anything. I want to trust in Your ability and not my own. Teach me to see difficulties in my life from Your perspective. Help me to focus on You and Your power. I want to be like Joshua and Caleb who believed in a good report and focused on You even in hard circumstances (Numbers 14:7-9). My responsibility is to carefully read, trust, and obey Your Word. Today I bring before You this difficulty in my life [*Name a hard situation you are right now facing*]. Help me not to fear but to trust You in this situation. I declare my faith in Your ability to fulfill Your promises to me. You will fight for me and win the battles in my life. You are mighty, powerful, righteous and true.

I have nothing to fear with You on my side. I will be strong and courageous even in hard times. I will not be terrified or discouraged, for the Lord my God will be with me wherever I go (**Joshua 1:9**). You will never leave me or forsake me (**Joshua 1:5**). I do not need to figure everything out. You already know the best plan for my life. I will not try any man-made method to do only what You can do. Show me Your supernatural power. Teach me how to walk by faith and pray breakthrough prayers. I choose to have faith in Your ability to break through every obstacle in my life. Just like Joshua, You will give me the land and every place where my feet step (**Joshua 1:3**) "Through you we push back our enemies; through your name we trample our foes. I do not trust in my bow, my sword does not bring me victory; but you give us victory over our enemies, you put our adversaries to shame. In God we make our boast all day long, and we will praise your name forever" (**Psalm 44:5-8**)

Lord, you have assigned me my portion and my cup; you have made my lot secure. The boundary lines have fallen for me in pleasant places; surely, I have a delightful inheritance. I will praise the Lord, who counsels me; even at night my heart instructs me. I have set the Lord always before me. Because he is at my right hand, I will not be shaken. Therefore, my heart is glad, and my tongue rejoices; my body also will rest secure, because you will not abandon me to the grave, nor will you let your Holy One see decay. You have made known to me the path of life; you will fill me with joy in your presence, with eternal pleasures at your right hand" (**Psalm 16:5-11**) In Jesus name, amen.

Chapter 7

His Word was True (God came through...)

The statement "His Word was True; God came through" can be seen in... **Isaiah 43:1-5;19**. Once you start trusting His word, it can be deeply impactful and transformative in your life. These verses from **Isaiah 43:1-5;19** convey powerful messages of God's faithfulness, protection, and promise of new beginnings. By internalizing and applying these words, individuals can find comfort, strength, and hope in their relationship with God.

Believing in the truth of God's promises and relying on His guidance can bring about a profound shift in perspective, leading to increased faith, resilience, and a renewed sense of purpose. It can inspire individuals to trust in God's plan, face challenges with confidence, and experience His blessings in their lives. Ultimately, the personal impact will depend on an individual's openness to embracing and living out these truths in their daily life.

We struggle and resort to depending on ourselves, others, and practically anything other than God sometimes and every single endeavor God uses to turn us back to Him. As we grow daily depending on God, we grow in trusting that He is most dependable, trustworthy, reliable, and faithful. He can be trusted to carry us through each day!

As we grow to fully rely on God, we must grow to trust Him as His Word.

Every word from God is true and can be trusted. We tend to put so much trust in earthly measures that we can find ourselves depending on God as a backup or last resort after something of this world has failed us. But we have Jesus' power at work within us! **Ephesians 3:20** and [21] tells us, "God is able to do immeasurably more than all you can ask or imagine according to his power at work within you."

Isaiah 43:1-5 NLT, The Savior of Israel, [1] But now, O Jacob, listen to the Lord who created you. O Israel, the one who formed you says, "Do not be afraid, for I have ransomed you. I have called you by name; you are mine. [2] When you go through deep waters, I will be with you. When you go through rivers of difficulty, you will not drown. When you walk through the fire of oppression, you will not be burned up; the flames will not consume you. [3] For I am the Lord, your God, the Holy One of Israel, your Savior. I gave Egypt as a ransom for your freedom; I gave Ethiopia and Seba in your place. [4] Others were given in exchange for you. I traded their lives for yours because you are precious to me. You are honored, and I love you. [5] "Do not be afraid, for I am with you. I will gather you and your children from east and west. [19] For I am about to do something new. See, I have already begun! Do you not see it? I will make a pathway through the wilderness. I will create rivers in the dry wasteland.

The statement mentioned from Isaiah 43:1-5;19 expresses a belief in God's faithfulness and intervention in our lives. For someone who embraces this belief, it can bring comfort, hope, and a sense of purpose. It can provide reassurance that God is with them, guiding and protecting them through life's challenges. This belief can instill confidence and courage, enabling individuals to face adversity with a renewed perspective. Ultimately, the impact of this statement on a person's life would depend on their personal faith and how they choose to interpret and apply it to their circumstances.

If God speaks something it WILL come to pass. "For with God nothing is ever impossible and no word from God shall be without power or impossible of fulfillment"- **Luke 1:37 AMP**

In the journey of faith, it is not uncommon for individuals to grapple with doubts and challenges regarding the reliability of God's Word and His faithfulness. Such uncertainties can arise from various sources, including personal experiences, philosophical dilemmas, or cultural influences. Addressing these concerns is essential for believers seeking to strengthen their relationship with God and deepen their understanding of His Word.

I for one had grappled with doubt over the fact that here I am a young believer who had been through so many different obstacles in life and now I'm at a place where everything and everyone around me had failed and I have to lean on God, but it just felt like the only voice I was hearing is that of the enemy.

Looking back now to when I was in that position, I've gotten to realize that the voice you hear and listen to the most is the voice that you will listen to when you are in your time of need. You tend to reflect on the negatives that you've been told or the bad experiences that you've been through.

Being rejected by my father and being told you have nothing and you're an outside child conceived out of what we would call in this day and age "a one-night stand", and you're a mistake and you were not planned like many other children around you were, these thoughts and feelings and negative words placed me in that state of Oppression, Depression, and I did not have any self-worth.

However, there was still a word that was spoken over my life, and I did not know how to trust and depend on the Word and use it against the lies of satan. In the book of Isaiah, it gives us a slight glimmer of hope that will guide us through the difficult phases in life.

God, Himself, stands over and watches over His own Word, making sure it is fulfilled.

Jeremiah 1:12 AMP says, "Then said the Lord to me, You have seen well, for I am alert and active, watching over My word to perform it."

- The KJV says, "For I will hasten my word to perform it."
- The NKJV says, "For I am ready to perform My word."
- The NIV says, "For I am watching to see that my word is fulfilled."
- The ERV says, "I am watching to make sure that my message to you comes true."

The Lord had spoken a word through my Spiritual Father the night after my water baptism at the age of 12. He said, "The Lord has a Great call on your life, and you will do great things for Him". We know that the enemy of our future, the devil, will always work overtime and send all the negatives our way, with the sole intended purpose of causing us to abort our purpose and dreams in God. This is exactly where I was in my life where the enemy was telling me I'm no good, nobody loves me, I'm a failure, I have no future. I listened to the voice in my head because of where I was in life and based on my relationship issues with my father, I believed the lies of the enemy.

I was ready to end it all, I was ready to jump off that bridge, I was ready to pull that trigger, I was ready to take those pills, BUT the Lord appeared to me and interrupted my plan of suicide. He said, *"I love you I'm with you and it's going to be ok".* Sometimes in life based on your situation all you need is a reassurance that everything will be ok. When your father, who should be your biggest motivator and protector, exempts himself from your life and you are left empty it's hard to trust. I had no other choice than to trust the Voice of God and when you put your trust in God the bible said, *"You shall be like Mount Zion a Mountain that's set on a hill that shall not be moved"*- **Psalm 125:1.**

"Everything was made by God; therefore, everything is sustained by God, determined by God, defined by God, including you and me. And therefore, we cannot know who we are without God." I was still learning about God, just newly saved I was not sure about His voice or the relationship He desired from me. I was broken, hurt, rejected and abandoned but there was something greater than the pain I was experiencing in my life that was hovering over me and that was the Word of God.

God's Word accomplishes that which He pleases, and purposes and it prospers in the thing for which He sent it.

[6] Seek, inquire for, and require the Lord while He may be found [claiming Him by necessity and by right]; call upon Him while He is near. [7] Let the wicked forsake his way and the unrighteous man his thoughts; and let him return to the Lord, and He will have love, pity, and mercy for him, and to our God, for He will multiply to him His abundant pardon. [8] For My thoughts are not your thoughts, neither are your ways My ways, says the Lord. [9] For as the heavens are higher than the earth, so are My ways higher than your ways and My thoughts than your thoughts. [10] For as the rain and snow come down from the heavens, and return not there again, but water the earth and make it bring forth and

sprout, that it may give seed to the sower and bread to the eater, [11] So shall My word be that goes forth out of My mouth: it shall not return to Me void [*without producing any effect, useless*], but it shall accomplish that which I please and purpose, and it shall prosper in the thing for which I sent it. - **Isaiah 55:6-11 AMP**

The rain and snow come down and water the earth and cause the seeds to sprout and grow up and produce fruit. In the same way, God's Word goes forth and produces good fruit. God's Word always produces a result – not just any result, but the exact result that God had for it. God's Word never returns to Him void – useless or without producing any effect - but it accomplishes that which He pleases, and purposes and it prospers in the thing for which He sent it! **Isaiah 55:11 NIV** says, "So is my word that goes out from my mouth: It will not return to me empty but will accomplish what I desire and achieve the purpose for which I sent it." The ERV says, "In the same way, my words leave my mouth, and they don't come back without results. My words make the things happen that I want to happen. They succeed in doing what I send them to do." The word of our God will stand and endure forever.

The grass withers, the flower fades, but the word of our God will stand forever- **Isaiah 40:8 AMP.** For all flesh (mankind) is like grass, and all its glory (honor) like [the] flower of grass. The grass withers and the flower drops off, [25] But the Word of the Lord (divine instruction, the Gospel) endures forever. And this Word is the good news which was preached to you. - **1 Peter 1:24-25 AMP**

The sum of Your word is truth [the total of the full meaning of all Your individual precepts]; and every one of Your righteous decrees endures forever. **Psalms 119:160 AMP**

God's Word will never pass away.

For assuredly, I say to you, till heaven and earth pass away, one jot or one tittle will by no means pass from the law till all is fulfilled. **Matthew 5:18 NKJV**

God is dependable and faithful to His Word.

So let us seize and hold fast and retain without wavering the hope we cherish and confess and our acknowledgement of it, for He Who promised is reliable (sure) and faithful to His word. **Hebrews 10:23 AMP**

The Word of God is tested, tried and proven.

As for God, His way is perfect; the word of the Lord is tried. He is a Shield to all those who trust and take refuge in Him. **2 Samuel 22:31 AMP**

As for God, His way is perfect! The word of the Lord is tested and tried; He is a shield to all those who take refuge and put their trust in Him. **Psalms 18:30 AMP**

Every word of God is tried and purified; He is a shield to those who trust and take refuge in Him. **Proverbs 30:5 AMP**

My Prayer for You

I pull down every evil imagination that stands against the knowledge of Christ and destroy the work of the devil over my mind, my spirit, my soul and my body by your blood, by your word, your fire and your anointing upon my life. Right now, I prophetically claim these words and I speak them over myself, my household and my loved ones. Now let the heavens bear me witness and let the earth hear and respond to the words that I speak into the atmosphere even now...In the mighty name of Jesus:

- I am unresponsive to demonic manipulation

- I am unresponsive to demonic oppression
- I am unresponsive to demonic suppression
- I am unresponsive to demonic attack
- I am more than I conqueror
- I refuse to be defeated or intimidated
- I have the mind of Christ and I love God with all of my heart
- I am a terror to the enemy and his cohorts
- I am strong, I am rich in every aspect of the term
- I am patient, I am kind, I have the nature of Christ in me and therefore I cannot be defeated.
- Thank you, Lord, for filling my day with your presence, your glory and your fire in my life, in Jesus mighty name.

Chapter 8

I Survived (So Can You)

My failures (School, Family, Marriage, Church, Ministry, Career, In Life)

(I know who I am and who's I am...)

Beloved, I pray that you may prosper in every way and [*that your body*] may keep well, even as [I know] your soul keeps well and prospers. **3 John 1:2 AMPC**

Survival in one definition is defined as- *Noun* : The state or fact of continuing to live or exist, typically in spite of an accident, ordeal, or difficult circumstances.

When I think of the word "survival" and attribute it to my personal life and I can say after all that I've gone through, taking a page out of the Apostle Paul's book where he said in-

Ephesians 6:13 AMP, Therefore, put on the complete armor of God, so that you will be able to [*successfully*] resist and stand your ground in the evil day [of danger], and having done everything [*that the crisis demands*], to stand firm [*in your place, fully prepared, immovable, victorious*].

I can stand today and say **I Survived and So Can You**. Looking back on the different phases of Test, Struggles, Ordeals, Difficult Circumstances, Labels and others own personal opinion of who I was and who I would become, I can now understand why I had to go through the vicissitudes of life.

In my meditation time one day I was thinking about life and what the everyday individual may go through; and while their going through the enemy who is as the scriptures says in John 8:44 "A liar, and the father of lies", wants you to think that you are all alone and no one else has gone through or is going through what you are going through.

He wants to Isolate you to destroy you, he wants you to believe no one cares, he wants you to believe no one understands, he wants you to believe that there's no other way out than to just give up, end your life, or be of no use to society.

Well, that's where I was and that's how I felt at the time when I was going through my different stages of challenges and struggles. I thought no one cared, no one understood, no one had the time to encourage me through what I was going through.

I was in a dark and lonely place, there were people around me but mentally I felt like I was alone in a dark world. Rejected from the womb, being brought forth in this world in what should have been an established family having a proud father and a loving mother but instead being born to a teenage, unprepared mother who didn't really intend to get pregnant ; however, at the age of 15 got pregnant and the fear of telling a mother who was expecting the best out of her... High School, University, and having a great Career, only for that to be altered because she got pregnant.

Not knowing what to do, or how to present it to her mother, being given advice to try abortion, the enemy intended to kill me from the womb, but I survived and discovered my Purpose and So Can You.

Having no mentor and guidance from a father I sought comfort in the streets of Dela Vega City, my community, and Spanish Town, hanging out with all the wrong crowds, getting involved in the wrong things, almost living out the name of who I was labeled as and almost committing murder at the age of 19 years old. I Survived and So Can You.

As I was sitting at my desk at work one day, something amazing happened to me that cemented the writing of this book "I Survived and So Can You". While sitting at my desk the spirit of the Lord said to get up and walk outside, I didn't understand why but I got up and went outside.

As soon as I walked down the steps and was walking in the parking lot, I heard a voice that said, 'Look down'. I looked and what I saw was an ant walking by himself with a big piece of food in its mouth. He was struggling but still walking to his destination. There were other ants passing by and he was struggling, and they did not stop to help.

The Spirit of the Lord spoke to me and told me that's where I was and that's where many people are today. We are carrying something bigger than us that's called Purpose. There are so many other people around us and they are passing us by seeing us struggling and won't offer help but God says what you are carrying is bigger than you and no one can carry it for you and all you have to do is Trust His Voice Through the Process as He guides you.

As I continued looking, I said to myself I'm going to help this ant because the food fell from its mouth, and it stopped. God said don't touch him because you will scare him off and cause him to run away from its purpose. Some of you have been touched by people who have caused you to run away from your purpose.

As I watched, the ant pick the food up again and kept on going because it was Intentional. I then saw a cigarette butt on the ground and the ant went under it and I said surely that's its destination. As I waited for a little while, I saw when it came out from the other side. I asked the Lord what this was and the Lord said to me that what I had experienced along my path of life was his purpose even though I went through the season of darkness.

When the ant went underneath the cigarette butt it was its season of darkness because the light of day was now blocked by the shadows of darkness from the cigarette butt. God said that's the same way on our journey in life to purpose. We will have those moments where the Light of Day will be Blocked by the Darkness of life and it seems like it's over, but the Lord said keep looking the Light is coming.

When the ant emerged from under the cigarette butt, he then went down into a hole because he had reached his destination. The Lord said, "Son, you went through your darkest moments of Rejection, Oppression, Depression and the darkest of them all Suicide." He said, "Just as the ant survived and made it to his destination was the same way you survived and gave birth to a ministry, Empowered to Win International Ministries with the support of your help mate Paula Davis-Smith.

My life was destined for the wrong path, and I did not know what was ahead for me. Oppressed and depressed at age 13 and almost jumping off that bridge to commit suicide, I was destined to fail and to die but God had a greater plan for my life as mentioned in **Jeremiah 29:11 NLT** [11] For I know the plans I have for you," says the Lord. "They are plans for good and not for disaster, to give you a future and a hope.

God had a Plan, He knew the end from the beginning, He is the Alpha and Omega, the Beginning and the End; He had a future for me, and He wanted to give me hope. I can truly look back today and say that I'm in the Survival Category. The state or fact of continuing to live or exist, typically in spite of an accident, ordeal, or difficult circumstances. In spite of all that I was facing I continued to live....

- In Spite of the Rejection from my father
- I continued to Live
- In Spite of people telling me I was an Accident
- I continued to Live
- In Spite of the Depression and Oppression I faced
- I continued to Live
- In Spite of feeling like I was in a world of sorrow all alone
- I continued to Live
- In Spite of the suicidal attempt on that bridge
- I continued to Live
- In Spite of the difficult circumstances
- I continued to Live

I continued to live because God had spoken a word over my life, and He knew that one day I would live to site and write my story and tell the world I Survived and So Can You.

I continued to live because God knew He would one day give me a revelation that "Someone has gone that way before", just as in the Bible from Genesis to Revelation everything that we could ever think of that's the most challenging thing in life, "Someone Has Gone That Way Before". He says someone has been through that before, and if they Survived So Can You.

I Survived My failures of School, not fully committing to the opportunity I had to obtain a great education.

I Survived My failures in the area of my Family, not having a father in my life to guide me as a young man through the stages of life, how to be a man, how to be ambitious, how to manage my finances, how to one day prepare to be a husband and father myself.

I Survived My failures in the areas of my Marriage where I made the mistakes and made the wrong choices and blamed others as to why I made the choice that were made.

I Survived My failures in Church, not fully committing as a young man to learn the word of God which would have been the Lamp to my feet and Light to my path.

I Survived My failures in my Career, because I didn't set myself up to have the proper education to obtain a well-paid job but rather settled for working in the laundry room of a nursing facility.

I Survived My failures In Life, so I can sit here today and tell the person who took the time to read this book today that no matter what you're currently going through, have gone through or will ever go through, "Never Give Up, God Will Make a Way Out of No Way". So, I encourage you today–

- Hope Like you've never Hoped Before
- Believe Like you've never Believed Before
- Trust Like you've never Trusted Before
- Pray Like you've never Prayed before
- And Survive the Process like you've never Survived before

Because I Survived, So Can You.

Numbers 6:24-26 AMPC [24] The Lord bless you and watch, guard, and keep you; [25] The Lord make His face to shine upon and enlighten you and be gracious (kind, merciful, and giving favor) to you; [26] The Lord lift up His [approving] countenance upon you and give you peace (tranquility of heart and life continually).

My Prayer for You as You Pray this Prayer

- I decree every curse over my life is reversed. I break through from prevailing and sustaining powers of darkness over this region in the name of Jesus.
- I arrest every demonic spirit through your word. Empower the angelic hosts to war in my behalf. I resist territorial strongholds.
- I sever ego-entanglements. Open the gates of psychological prisons and deliver us from the spirits of shame, embarrassment, harassment, iniquity.
- Deliver us from the spirit of strongholds and pride.
- Deliver me from stigmatization, emotional blackmail, social impediments, seductions, satanic limitations, satanic illusions, addictions, demonic restriction, cultural entrenchments, cultic stronghold, bewitchments, traditions, anti-Christ cultural environments.
- Free me from limitations, handicaps, impediments. I refuse to be marginalized, stigmatized, immobilized, terrorized, characterized, criticized, tolerated, censored, misjudged, mishandled, mismanagement.

- I wear a cloak of favor. I disengage demonic triggers and psychological buttons. I short circuit them.
- I am nonresponsive to demonic oppression. I establish my superior authority over this region by the blood, the word, by the Spirit of God.
- For this reason, I remind you that the son of God was made manifest that He would destroy the works of the devil. I decree that the works of the devil are destroyed.
- It is destroyed over this region, it is destroyed over my neighborhood, it is destroyed over my body, over my family, over my children, over my loved ones, over my ministry, over my pastor, over my doctor and lawyer, over my government.
- The evil works of the devil is destroyed. I declare and decree that the plans and the purposes of God shall prevail.
- The word of God prevails. Hallelujah! His will prevails. My prophetic purpose and destiny prevail. My vision prevails. My business prevails. My ideas prevail.
- I prophecy to the four winds, that things that have died prematurely and dried up because of satanic activities are quickened and come to life.
- I declare that the pieces of my destiny and financial ministerial relational puzzle: it comes together. My life comes together.
- I decree that my money is coming together, Hallelujah! My business is coming together. My relationships are coming together. My family is coming together.

- The body of Christ is coming together. My ministry is coming together. My marriage, my family are coming together. My budget is coming together.
- Our governments are coming together. Our leaderships are coming together.
- Everything is working together according to your will. Father I thank you, with you nothing is impossible, so therefore, Father I decree and declare, hallelujah, that the flood gates of heaven are opened. Let it rain.
- Spirit of God usher us into times of refreshing that you promised will come from the presence of God. I decree and declare that there shall be no more demonic droughts, no more demonic dryness, distress, disease, depression and no more demonic drama.
- We come in the volume of the book it is written of us. We come in the power of God, the God of Joshua- Hallelujah!
- We decree and declare that every impenetrable wall must come down in the name of Jesus and in the power of the most High God.
- I shatter barriers, blockages, barricades, and boulders. I declare that I am advancing to the calling, to the purposes and the plan to God.

Places and the Materials The Enemy used in trying to take my life

Photo 1

Photo 2

Photo 3

Photo 4

Photo 5

Photo 6

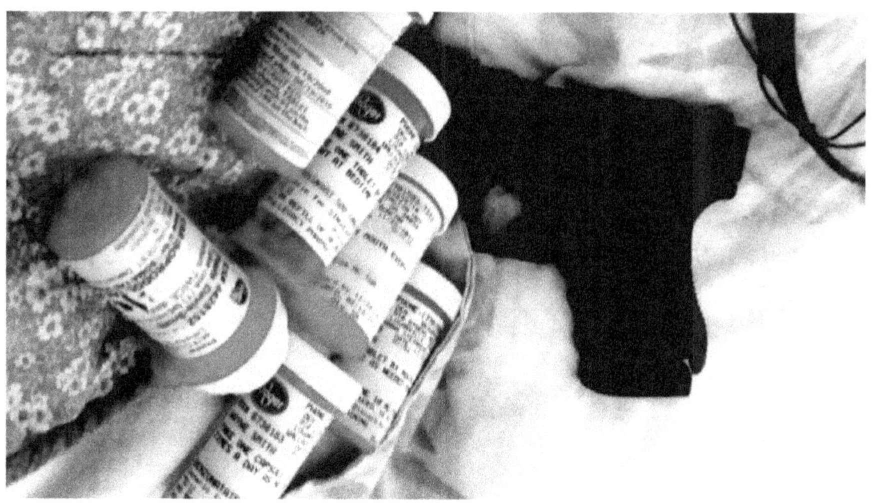

Photo 7

AUTHOR BIO

Bishop Wayne A. Smith Sr. is in his ninth year serving as the overseer and presiding Bishop of Empowered to Win International Ministries in Stone Mountain, GA.

Born and raised in Spanish Town, St. Catherine, Jamaica, he's the oldest of four siblings. He gave his life to the Lord at the age of twelve and received the gift of the Holy Spirit after his water baptism. He migrated to the United States as a teenager and faithfully served the Lord. He served many years in ministry in different capacities, including as a youth leader and evangelist, before being called to start his ministry with his wife.

In early 2007, a prophetic word was spoken over his life: God was calling him to be an international evangelist. Heeding to the will of God, on January 20, 2013, he gave birth. He hosted his first-ever conference, *Empowered to*

Win on international grounds in George Town, Grand Cayman Islands. The Lord opened the doors to the Island of Barbados, and in August of that same year, he hosted his 2nd Conference in Barbados. As a result of his faithfulness, the ministry of Empowered to Win International Ministries, a vision bestowed upon him by the Lord, started on November 22, 2013.

Bishop Wayne's ministry is a testament to his versatility and dedication. He has a deliverance ministry, preaching with an anointing that destroys the enemy's yoke. He holds ordination as a Bishop and has served in various roles, including Pastor, Evangelist, International Speaker, Revivalist, Youth Motivator, and Author. His ministry is marked by an Evangelistic and Prophetic anointing, further empowered by the gift of the Holy Spirit.

He oversees two ministries in his current assignment season: Empowered to Win Ministries, Canada, and Rhema Global Impact Ministries, Cayman Islands. He considers it a profound blessing to serve others. Embracing the responsibilities of a Bishop, which include teaching, governing, and sanctifying, he is an ardent worshipper dedicated to following the will of the Lord with unwavering vigor, strength, and determination. His message to those encountering challenges is one of resilience: "Never give up; God will pave a way even amid seemingly insurmountable obstacles."

Bishop Wayne currently serves alongside his wife, Senior Pastor Paula Davis-Smith. Despite his demanding schedule, Bishop Wayne exemplifies a Godly father, always willing to listen and give Godly instructions and support for church and home. Married for over 28 years to Senior Pastor Paula Davis-Smith, they are blessed with two wonderful children: Wayne A Smith Jr. and Abigail A. Smith.